This Book Belongs To:

....

I am a student at

....

MY FIRST BOOK
of COLLEGE

MEMORIES, MILESTONES & MISHAPS

ILLUSTRATED BY MARSHA A. GRILL

Front Porch Press

Published by Front Porch Press, 1724 Vassar Drive, Lansing, Michigan 48912
Phone: (517) 487-9295. Fax: (517) 487-0888. E-mail: styler@voyager.net

ISBN 0-9656086-3-8

Acknowledgements

We would like to thank Craig McCool, Kelly O'Connor, Cheryl Rilly, and Lisa Scriver for contributing their wit and humor; Marci Jacobs and Jeff Fillion for graphic design and editing; Jennifer Braselton, Kim Broviac, Andrea and Mike Cirrito, Judy Eyde, Richard Galosy, Millie Gilin, Joyce Kareti, Pat Sladek and, of course, Gary Tyler for their continuing support and suggestions.

ARRIVAL DAY!

Date of arrival:_____

Time of arrival:_____ *a.m.* *p.m.*   Parking space found:_____ *a.m.* *p.m.*

Delivered by: ❑ Parents   ❑ Friend   ❑ Hitchhiked

Height:_____ *with Doc Martens*   Weight:_____ *with quarters for laundry*
_____ *without Doc Martens*   _____ *without quarters for laundry*

Color of Hair:_____

Distinguishing Characteristics: *(provide location and/or description)*

Tattoos: *(permanent)*_____   Piercings: *(on purpose)*_____
*(washable)*_____   *(accidental)*_____

Dorm:_____   Room #:_____

Tuition:_____
Room/Board:_____
Books:_____

TOTAL DEBT:_____

_____

```
┌─ ─ ─ ─ ─ ─ ─ ─ ─ ─ ─ ─ ─ ─ ─ ─ ┐



│                                 │


                place photo here

│                                 │



└─ ─ ─ ─ ─ ─ ─ ─ ─ ─ ─ ─ ─ ─ ─ ─ ┘
```

Proud Parent(s)

Mom's parting words of wisdom:

_____

_____

_____

_____

_____

Dad's parting words of wisdom:

_____

_____

(Dad slipped me $_____ I expected $_____)

My bedroom was converted into_____

MOVING IN!

My check list:

Stuff I brought:

___TV *(300 watts)*

___VCR *(20 watts)*

___Carpet

___Refrigerator *(500 watts)*

___CD player *(1000 watts)*
    w/surround sound

___DVD *(20 watts)*

___Full length mirror

___Computer *(600 watts)*

___Fax/Scanner *(800 watts)*

___Floor lamp *(300 watts)*

___La-Z-Boy

___Black light *(100 watts)*

___Loft

___Desk lamp *(150 watts)*

___Bicycle

___Blender *(350 watts)*

___Cappuccino maker *(1100 watts)*

___Pillows/linens

___Weights/Bench

___Electric razor *(20 watts)*

___Bulletin board

___Milk crates

___Strobe light *(100 watts)*

___Printer *(1800 watts)*

Y N
❏ ❏ My room has more than one electrical outlet.

More stuff I brought...

___Microwave *(1000 watts)*

___Lava lamp *(250 watts)*

___Futon

___Xmas lights *(60 watts)*

___Bathroom scale

___Papason

___PlayStation™ *(50 watts)*

___Shelves

___Fan *(60 watts)*

___Comforter

___Stuffed animals

___Curling iron *(1500 watts)*

___CD rack

___Posters

___Aquarium *(200 watts)*

___Hair dryer *(2000 watts)*

___Heater for pet snake *(60 watts)*

___Stairmaster

___Iron *(1200 watts)*

___Hockey equipment

___Roller blades

_____**TOTAL TONNAGE**

_____**TOTAL WATTS**

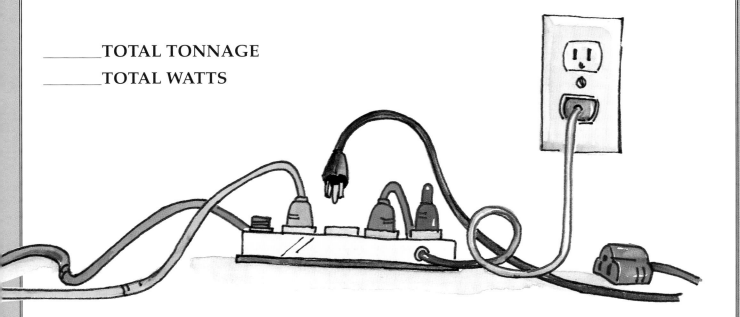

THE ULTIMATE DORM ROOM

…And *my* room

. . . most days

place photo here

place photo here

Parent's Weekend

Roommate Chemistry

Me		My Roommate
	Neatness Quotient *ie, Martha Stewart/Pig Pen*	
	Temperament *ie, High/Low Maintenance*	
	Smoker/Non-smoker	
	Favorite CD *ie, Dixie Chicks/Puff Daddy*	
	Pizza Toppings	
	Software *PC/Mac*	
	Letterman/Leno	
	Funding *Mom & Dad/Pell & Stafford*	
	Favorite Snacks *Celery Sticks/Pizza Sticks*	
	Skinny Latté/Bud Lite	
	Sleep Schedule *Early Bird/Night Owl*	
	BMW/Bus	
	Study Habits *Diligent/None*	
	Politics *Right Wing/Left Wing* *"Chicken wing, anyone?"*	

MY ROOMMATE

Name_____

  *a.k.a. (nickname)*_____

Hometown/Planet_____

  *Photo □ *does*
         □ *doesn't* resemble actual person

place photo here

* Roomie's Senior Pic

The biggest brawl we've ever had_____
_____
_____

The physical trait or personal habit he/she'd pay me not to divulge_____
_____
_____

The outfit he/she always wears when trying to be cool_____
_____
_____

The dumbest/funniest/weirdest thing he/she's ever said or done_____
_____
_____

My favorite thing to "borrow" when he/she's gone _____

_____

_____

The best secret he/she's ever told me _____

_____

_____

The prank that traumatized him/her the most _____

_____

_____

_____

_____

Our unresolved "issues" _____

_____

_____

_____

ISSUES:
Toenail
Clippings ✔
Overnight
Guests ✔
Yogurt Gone ✔

VITAL INFORMATION

This is me.

(right thumb print)

insert student I.D. here

(left thumb print)

G.P.A._____   S.A.T._____   A.C.T._____   D.N.A._____

(real or imagined)

My PINS, etc.

ATM_____   Phone Card_____   Dad's AMEX Platinum_____

VISA_____   Email Account_____   _____

MasterCard_____   Computer Access Code_____   _____

These *could* also be me . . .

Valid Driver's License

(insert here)

a.k.a.

a.k.a.

a.k.a.

a.k.a.

a.k.a.

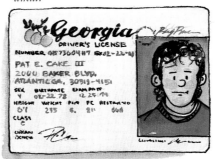

17

NOW I KNOW MY ABC'S

A is for ATM

B . . . _____

C . . . the *CURVE!*

D . . . a grade my parents won't pay for

E . . . e-mail

F . . . another grade my parents won't pay for.

G . . . _____

H . . . happy hour

I . . . 'Insufficient Funds'

J . . . a *JOB!*

K . . . Kinko's™

L . . . _____

M . . . _____

N . . . nipple, nose, and navel rings

O . . . overstudied (yeah, *riiight!*)

P . . . procrastination

Q . . . Quiz ? *What quiz*?!?

R . . . _____

S . . . Spring Break

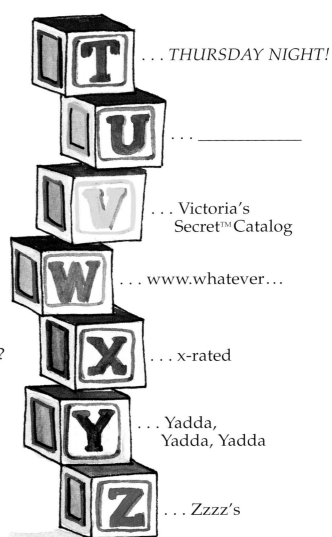

T . . . *THURSDAY NIGHT!*

U . . . _____

V . . . Victoria's Secret™ Catalog

W . . . www.whatever…

X . . . x-rated

Y . . . Yadda, Yadda, Yadda

Z . . . Zzzz's

FIRSTS

Sucks   Awesome

1 2 3 4 5 6 7 8 9 10

My first day of class: I'd give it a_____

(Circle where appropriate)
awesome, kinda cool, overwhelming, confusing, exciting, nerve-racking,
interesting, boring, "I'm in the wrong place!"

_____

_____

_____

_____

_____

Largest lecture:_____   How many times I got lost:_____

TOTAL NUMBER OF PAGES ASSIGNED:_____

Sucks   Awesome

1 2 3 4 5 6 7 8 9 10

My first paper: I'd give it a_____

(Circle where appropriate)
*brilliant, pretty good, interesting, confusing, unintelligible, late,
written by roommate, downloaded from the Internet*

Topic:_____

_____

_____

THE PROFESSOR GAVE IT A:_____

My first exam: I'd give it a _____

(Circle where appropriate)
*easy, predictable, unpredictable, unfair, impossible, confusing, too long,
nothing looked even remotely familiar, "Is this guy kidding?"*

Course_____   I studied_____hours

_____

_____

THE PROFESSOR GAVE IT A:_____

My first party: I'd give it a _____

(Circle where appropriate)
awesome, kinda cool, overwhelming, confusing, fun, exciting, boring,
interesting,"I'm in the wrong place!", "I don't remember…"

Location_____   Number of attendees_____

Refreshments_____

_____

_____

_____

_____

THE POLICE OFFICER GAVE IT A:_____

I KNOW MY NUMBERS

Pizza......................................Tel._____

TicketMaster™.............................Tel._____

Yellow Cab™...............................Tel._____

Overdraft Hotline.........................Tel._____

Soap Update Hotline......................Tel._____

Psychic Friends™.........................Tel._____

Loveline™..................................Tel._____

Molly Maid™..............................Tel._____

Exterminator..............................Tel._____

Contagious Disease Center..............Tel._____

Bail Bondsman............................Tel._____

Legal Aid..................................Tel._____

Dial-a-Prayer.............................Tel._____

LOOK HOW MUCH I'VE GROWN

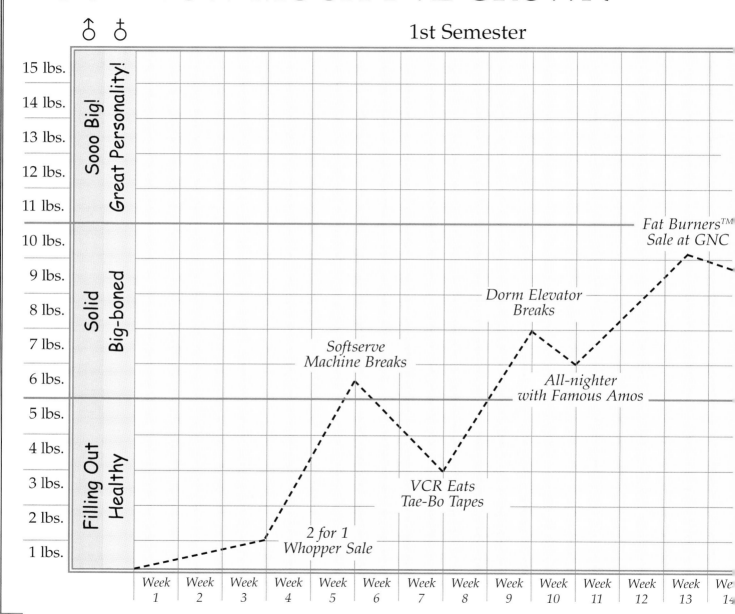

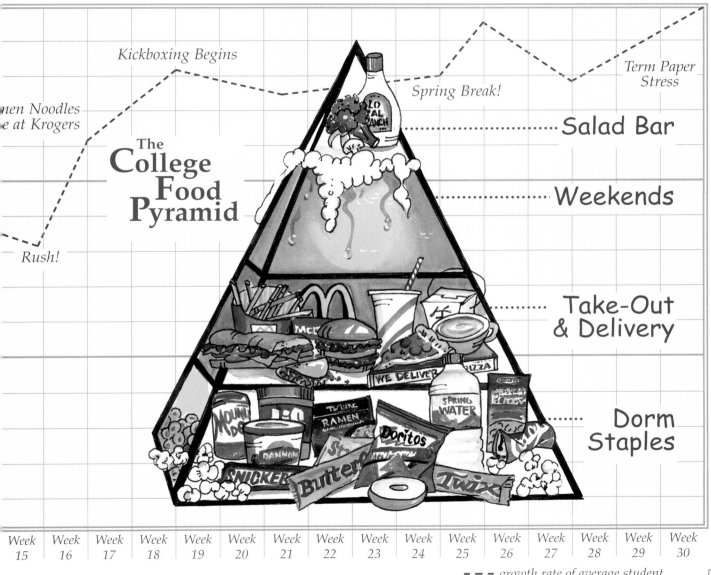

Kickboxing Begins

Term Paper
Stress

nen Noodles
e at Krogers

The
College
Food
Pyramid

Salad Bar

Spring Break!

Weekends

Rush!

Take-Out
& Delivery

WE DELIVER

Dorm
Staples

| Week 15 | Week 16 | Week 17 | Week 18 | Week 19 | Week 20 | Week 21 | Week 22 | Week 23 | Week 24 | Week 25 | Week 26 | Week 27 | Week 28 | Week 29 | Week 30 |

- - - *growth rate of average student*

MY FAVORITE PEOPLE

- ❏ TA's who speak English.

- ❏ Dads who build lofts.

- ❏ Kids who lower the curve.

- ❏ Profs who never change their exams.

- ❏ Greeks with test files.

- ❏ Guys into computers—who will fix mine.

- ❏ Anyone 21.

- ❏ R.A.'s who don't mind a party as long as they're invited.

- ❏ Secretaries who will change class schedules.

- ❏ Advisers who'll sign anything.

- ❏ "Townies"… with mom's who cook and a washer and dryer that doesn't need quarters.

- ❏ Bouncers who can't add.

- ❏ Lab partners who do all the work.

- ❏ People who never miss class— AND will share their notes.

- ❏ Grandmas who send care packages.

- ❏ Grandpas who send cash.

- ❏ Anyone who understands calculus!

- ❏ _____

- ❏ _____

MY BEST EXCUSES

For:

Cutting class_____
_____
_____

Late papers_____
_____
_____

Dropping courses after the drop date *(Tip: Obituaries help)*_____
_____
_____

The charges on my parents' phone card_____
_____
_____

Hitting on my roommates date_____
_____
_____

The smell coming from our room_____
_____
_____

Asking my parents for more money_____
_____
_____

Trashing my roommates favorite sweater_____
_____
_____

Bank overdrafts_____
_____
_____
_____

The keg in the shower_____
_____
_____
_____

KEEPSAKES

Lock of hair from

- ☐ the campus "babe"
- ☐ prof's comb-over
- ☐ the team mascot
- ☐ cafeteria meatloaf
- ☐ _____

Buy-back refund for books

Ticket stubs

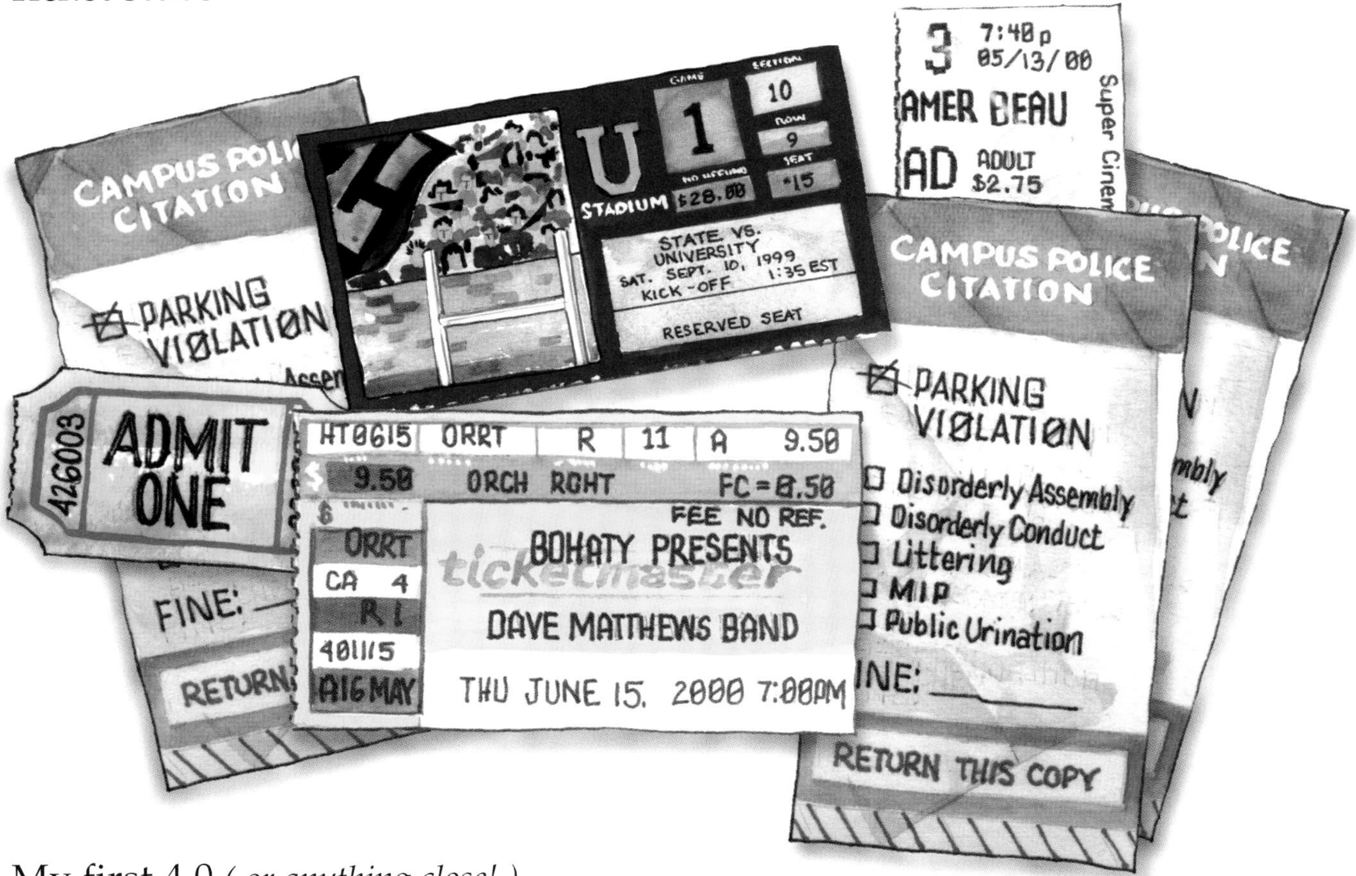

My first 4.0 *(or anything close!)*

NURSERY RHYMES

Ramen noodles hot,
Mac'n cheese cold
Bagels with cream cheese—
Hold the mold
Pop-Tarts and cereal,
Oatmeal, rolled
Whatever's in the fridge is
Nine days old!

Pat-a-cake,
Pat-a-cake,
Pizza Man
Bring us a pizza
As fast as you can!
Pepperoni,
Mushrooms, extra cheese,
This time the check won't bounce,
PLEASE, PLEASE, PLEASE!

Wee Willie Winkie ran through the dorm
Upstairs and downstairs, midnight to morn
Shouting through the hallways,
Leaving none to rest
O.D.'ed on NoDoz—
Then slept through the test.

Little Boy Blue, turn off your alarm!
You should've known better than go to the bar
Now it's morning—your class you'll not make
For you're high in your loft with a huge headache!

To Jamaica, to Cancun, it's time for Spring Break!
We all need some fun and a tan that's not fake
We'll rock to the tunes and sleep until noon
Then home again, home again
Way to soon!

Rub-a-dub-dub
Who's turn to clean the tub?
The green stuff's beginning to grow…
With the tuition we've paid
Isn't there a maid?
Maybe we'll just have to mow…

Tweedledum on Tweedledee did
pull a nasty caper
For Tweedledum had wickedly copied
'Dee's term paper
So just when Tweedledum thought he was headed for the Dean's List
Squealed Tweedledee "He copied me!"
And "Dum" was instead dismissed.

It's raining, it's pouring
My roommate's still snoring
Got toasted last night and into a fight
And we bailed him out this morning.

Twinkle, twinkle little star
We all know you will go far
Your GPA's so very high
Employers will surely offer the sky
You've done it all, it must be great
We're trying hard to emulate—
Such deeds, though, are tough to repeat…
Think we could have your old cheat sheets???

ATM, ATM,
Won't you come 'on line'
I need some cash for my library fine—
$50 for the HOLD card,
$50 for my date
And $50 for the house dues
I'm always paying late!

MY MOMMY AND DADDY LOVE ME

Even when…

- ❏ the U-Haul isn't big enough.

- ❏ they have to pay for a class I 'forgot' to drop.

- ❏ 4.0 is my bank balance and not my GPA.

- ❏ I'm less than the perfect role model during 'Siblings Weekend.'

- ❏ all of my long distance calls are 'billed to a third number'… *theirs.*

- ❏ I'm majoring in art history instead of something "that pays."

- ❏ the only package I bring home for the holidays is my dirty laundry.

- ❏ I dropped out of school 'to find myself' and I'm still lost.

- ❏ I scored more points in the dorm Sega challenge than on my math final.

❑ everything I own is in the middle of the garage for the entire summer.

❑ my campus parking tickets are more than tuition.

❑ I maxed out three credit cards.

❑ my roommate sued me for a lost sweater on Judge Judy.

❑ I used our family as a case study in Psych. 101.

❑ *MY GRADES ARRIVE!!!*

❑ _____

❑ _____

❑ _____

TOILET TRAINING

You've had one bathroom, maybe two or three, at your disposal your entire life, eh? Never given it much thought, I'll bet— until now. All of a sudden it's like **'Whoa—community bathrooms?!?'**

To help you overcome the initial horror of realizing that your daily personal hygiene regimen (if you have one) and grossest bodily functions will be performed in unison with fifty or so complete strangers (there were never pictures of that in the catalog, eh?), the following "syllabus" of basic etiquette and technique will help you meet the upcoming (or outgoing) challenge with grace and style.

POTTY PRINCIPLE #1: EVERYBODY DOES IT.

You know that gorgeous Jennifer Aniston look-alike down the hall; the little princess who thinks her poop doesn't stink? Well, guess what? It does. And that's the point. Everybody's does. Nobody's gonna hold it against you so don't hold it against them. In fact, don't 'hold it' at all!

POTTY PRINCIPLE #2: PICKING YOUR SEAT

The goal here is to secure a reasonably hygienic, eruption-free perch. There's nothing worse than taking the rap for someone else's potty indiscretions. So, in addition to checking paper supply, lock function, and seat condition, peer into the bowl itself. Avoid any containing foreign objects or emitting strange odors (yes, sniff!). It is likely that they are still in recovery phase—and flooding or a virtual avalanche may be imminent with the added stress of even the lightest "load."

POTTY PRINCIPLE #3:
KEEPING A LID ON IT

There will be times when you have really 'big plans' and would prefer a little privacy to complete the mission. This calls for a "fly-by." Walk in, fake a nose blow or a hair check and survey the scene. If 'all's clear' you're free to poop in peace. If not, come back later. However, be careful not to become a "frequent flyer." Too many "fly-bys" start to look suspicious.

POTTY PRINCIPLE #4:
ATTITUDE IS EVERYTHING

Occasionally, your plans for "discreet do-do" may be foiled—you've stunk up the place and you're totally caught. Just hold your head high and continue exchanging pleasantries. Don't ever acknowledge a smell even exists unless you can blame it on someone else.

Comments like "Omigod, it smells like someone died in here?" readily shift the blame to a phantom pooper.

POTTY PRINCIPLE #5:
AVOID PICKING UP NEW "FRIENDS"

A word about showers. No one but a biology major is interested in learning exactly what that yucky stuff is that's growing in them, but on the outside chance that it may be flesh-eating you're gonna want to avoid it. The answer—shoes! Wear 'em in the shower. Not only will they insulate your tootsies from the fungal array, but for you ladies, they'll enhance your balance. Yep, shaving your legs without coming into contact with slime-covered walls is quite some feat. It requires agility and creativity. In fact, let me suggest the 'jack-knife' position. Simply bend over and grab your ankles for support (uh … ignore this part, guys) and shave away. Remember, however, to stand up periodically as the jackknife has been known to cause dizziness. Better yet, forget shaving altogether.

So, now you know—coeds going 'au natural' has nothing to do with the women's movement, it's coordination!

POTTY PRINCIPLE #6:
BEWARE OF PARTY-POOPERS

Enter at your own risk—and don't inhale. Yep, it's 2:00 a.m. on any given Friday or Saturday night. The "john's" a-jump'n with tummies turnin' and partiers poopin'. The EPA has not sanctioned some of the things you're going to see and SMELL in this environment. Nothing contagious here, but you might find a nearby gas station rest room more appealing—or, at least, less likely to induce the gag reflex.

POTTY PRINCIPLE #7: BONUS!

Still a little disheartened about communal living? Here's the upside: There's no better place on campus to get the "poop" than in the john. We're talking networking! Yes indeed, community bathrooms are about sharing and in

between the brushing and flushing, you're going to hear it all—who's the best Prof, where's the best party, what essays are on the Humanities final, and what web site has the cheapest downloadable term papers. Trust me, it pays to linger (as opposed to lurk) a while and just 'shoot the shit' as they say.

A word of caution, however—you never know who's in the next stall. So if you're there to let 'er rip about your roommate's idiosyncrasies or sordid sex life, make sure there are no familiar feet within earshot. The "Oh, I was talking about a different Alicia who weighs more than Rhode Island…" doesn't always cut it.

So there you have it. Good luck and GO in peace.

I LIKE TO COLOR

Our football helmets look like this

Our basketball jerseys look like this

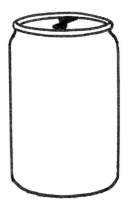

My favorite beverage looks like this

41

ONCE UPON A TIME
Tales of disbelief and wonder...

Spring Break _____
_____
_____
_____
_____
_____
_____
_____

Tailgate _____
_____
_____
_____
_____
_____
_____
_____
_____

Road Trip _____
_____
_____
_____
_____
_____

Thursday Night_____
_____
_____
_____
_____
_____
_____

Friday Night_____
_____
_____
_____
_____
_____
_____

Saturday Night_____
_____
_____
_____
_____
_____
_____

PHOTO-OPS

My bike before it was stolen…

The shower… clean!

My roommate when least expecting it…

"Is there a problem officer?"

Uh… my study group?

My R.A. in breach of the Code of Conduct!

MY FAVORITE GAME

Pledge Week

What is the period of time when you finally dust your furniture?

Eenie, meenie, miney, moe

How did you select your major?

The Library

If your parents call, where should I tell them you've gone?

Cramming

What is the method for placing laundry in the dorm washer and dryer when it costs $2 per load?

Bacterium Pneumosyliacoccus

To what Family does the green fuzz in your cereal bowl belong?

The Unabomber

Who is the only roommate worse than mine?

JEOPARDY!

A baseball cap and Tic Tacs™

What is an acceptable substitute for daily grooming?

Credit hours

What is the time period when the ATM is accessible?

The most expensive T-shirt you'll ever own

What comes free with every credit card you sign up for?

2 A.M. feeding

What is another name for 'last call' at Taco Bell?

A college student who mispronounces your name, won't take 'no' for an answer, and calls at dinner time

What is a Telemarketer?

27 consecutive days

How long has my roommate worn the same jeans without washing them?

LETTERS HOME

✂ ---- *(Cut and mail as is, or modify to fit your circumstances.)* ---- ✂

Dear Mom and Dad,

Sorry it has taken me so long to write to you but so much has been happening here and I really didn't want you to worry. You may want to sit down for this, really.

Are you sitting?

Well, then, I am getting along quite well now. The skull fracture and concussion I got when I jumped out of the window of my dormitory when it caught fire is pretty well healed. I only spent two weeks in the hospital and now I can see almost normally and only get those sick headaches once a day.

Fortunately, the fire in the dorm and my jump was witnessed by an attendant at the nearby gas station. He was the one who called the Fire Department and the ambulance. He also visited me in the hospital and since I had nowhere to live because of the burned-out dorm, he was kind enough to invite me to share his apartment with him. It's really a basement room, but it is kind of cute. He is a very fine boy and we have fallen deeply in love and are planning on getting married. We haven't got the exact date yet, but it will be before my pregnancy begins to show. Yes, mom and dad, I am pregnant. I know how much you are looking forward to being grandparents and I know that you will welcome the baby and give it the same love and devotion you gave me when I was a child. The reason for the delay in our marriage is that my boyfriend has a minor infection which prevents us from passing our premarital blood tests and I carelessly caught it from him.

He is kind, and, although not well educated and of a different race and religion I know you will welcome him into our family with open arms.

Now that I have brought you up to date, I want to tell you that there was no fire, nor am I pregnant nor infected nor anything else. However, I am getting D in Calculus and F in Chemistry and I want you to see those marks in their proper perspective.

Your loving daughter,
(your name)

I CAN DRESS MYSELF

MY LISTS

Nasty foods to avoid in the cafeteria

Hot Profs/TA's
1.
2.
3.
4.
5.

Tattoos I'm considering...

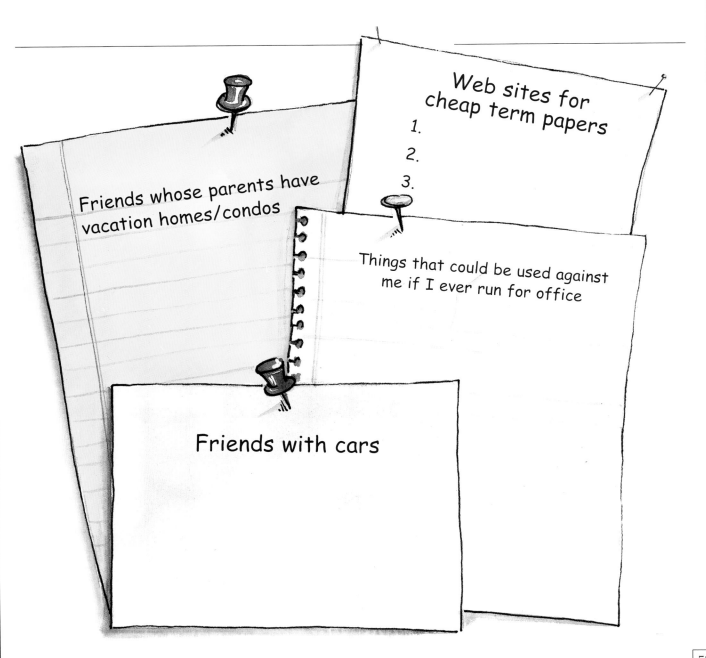

FINALS

Multiple Choice *(circle appropriate answer)* **4 PTS. EA.**

1. The best improvement to your dorm room has been
   a. Adding sub-woofers to the computer speakers
   b. Cleaning
   c. Locking my roommate out
   d._____

2. I attend class
   a. Always
   b. Most of the time
   c. When the weather is good
   d._____

3. The reason I dropped my class was
   a. Too much reading
   b. Too much writing
   c. They actually expected me to be there
   d._____

4. I made the college newspaper
   a. The Dean's list
   b. Personals
   c. Crime Beat
   d._____

Quantitative Reasoning *(solve the equation)*

$$\frac{\text{Hours of Study}}{\text{Hours of Exams}} \quad X \quad \frac{\text{Tuition}}{\text{G.P.A.}} \quad = \quad \underline{\hspace{5cm}}$$

Effective Cost of Education

10 PTS.

True/False *(circle appropriate answer)*

4 PTS. EA.

1. T F   My grades are better than they were in high school

2. T F   The pants that fit at mid-terms still fit by finals

3. T F   My roommates girlfriend/boyfriend uses my toothbrush more than I do

4. T F   I love having my parents call—especially on Sunday mornings!

5. T F   My closet becomes a "free-for-all" when I leave for the weekend

6. T F   I never have a problem getting the courses I want or need

7. T F   I pick up extra cash by selling blood

Fill in the Blank *(score 2 pt. per answer)* **30 PTS.**

1. **My favorite…**
   Professor_____
   Course_____
   Coffee shop to study in_____
   Sitcom_____
   Pub_____

2. **My coolest…**
   Door decoration_____
   Dance move_____
   Halloween costume_____
   Fashion statement_____

3. **My best…**
   Music to study by_____
   Grade_____
   Place to get free food_____
   Place to pick up guys/girls_____

4. **My biggest…**
   Waste of time_____
   Waste of money_____
   Challenge_____
   Phone bill_____

Essay

20 PTS.

1. If I could do the first year over, I would_____
    _____
    _____
    _____
    _____
    _____

2. The best part of college so far has been_____
    _____
    _____
    _____
    _____

_____**TOTAL POINTS**

BONUS POINTS: Total number of credits earned

—— Total number of CD's lost

PACKING UP

Stuff lost, loaned, pawned, or otherwise missing:

_____   _____   _____
_____   _____   _____
_____   _____   _____
_____   _____   _____

Stuff I don't know how I got:

_____   _____   _____
_____   _____   _____
_____   _____   _____

Stuff my parents won't let me bring home:

_____   _____
_____   _____

Achievements

☐ Damage deposit returned in full.

☐ I will be allowed to return in the fall.

Wave Bye-Bye!

NOTES

MY GLOSSARY

Advanced Placement: moving the garbage bag closer to the door

Catalog: a book from which you select courses rather than merchandise. Similar to Neiman-Marcus, only more expensive.

Campus Newspaper: a good substitute for toilet tissue

Community Bathroom: the closest you'll ever come to living in a third world country

Drops and Adds: pounds you gain and lose during the semester

Elective: a fresh pair of underwear

Lectures: something you get from your parents after your third incomplete

Midterms: the point at which your spending money for the entire semester is gone

Orientation: that which you struggle to regain after your first all-nighter

Schedule Conflict: when a course in which attendance is taken falls at the same time as your favorite "soap"